The Ultimate Resilience Building Plans

A Practical Guide to Understanding and Surviving Disasters

By

Susan J. Wisner

Table of Content

INTRODUCTION

Understanding the Need for Disaster Preparedness

In an increasingly unpredictable world, the ability to effectively respond to and recover from disasters is crucial.From natural calamities like earthquakes and floods to unnatural events such as industrial accidents,wars and terrorism, disasters can strike without warning and disrupt lives profoundly. The reality is that while we cannot always prevent these events, we can significantly improve our chances of survival and recovery through proper preparation and knowledge.

The Importance of Being Prepared

Disaster preparedness is not merely about stockpiling supplies or knowing the location of the nearest emergency shelter; it involves a comprehensive understanding of potential threats, strategic planning, and proactive measures. It is about developing a resilient mindset and cultivating skills that will enable you to navigate through crises effectively. This manual aims to equip you with the knowledge and tools needed to handle various disaster scenarios with confidence.

Scope and Purpose of the Manual

"The Ultimate Resilience Building Plans: A Practical Guide to Understanding and Surviving Disasters" is designed to serve as an all-encompassing resource for individuals, families, and communities seeking to enhance their disaster preparedness and response capabilities. Whether you are new to disaster planning or looking to refine your existing strategies, this guide offers valuable insights and actionable steps for a wide range of disaster situations.

What You Will Find in This Manual

Comprehensive Coverage

The manual delves into 14 different types of disasters, including natural events like hurricanes and wildfires, as well as unnatural events such as terrorism and industrial accidents. Each chapter provides a detailed examination of the specific challenges associated with these events and offers practical advice on how to prepare and respond effectively.

Actionable Steps

Each chapter is structured to provide clear, actionable steps that you can take to enhance your preparedness and improve your response. From assembling survival kits to developing evacuation plans, you will find practical tips that are easy to implement and tailored to different types of disasters.

Expert Advice and Real-World Scenarios: Drawing on insights from disaster management experts and real-world case studies, the manual offers expert advice and practical examples that illustrate key concepts and strategies. This approach helps to bridge the gap between theory and practice, making it easier for you to apply the information in real-life situations.

Focus on Recovery and Resilience

In addition to preparing for and responding to disasters, this manual emphasizes the importance of recovery and resilience. It provides guidance on how to manage the aftermath of a disaster, including financial recovery, rebuilding efforts, and psychological support.

Why This Manual Matters

Disasters can have devastating effects on individuals and communities, leading to loss of life, injury, and significant disruptions. However, being well-prepared can make a critical difference in how you handle these challenges. By equipping yourself with the right knowledge and tools, you can reduce the impact of disasters on your life and increase your chances of a successful recovery.

How to Use This Manual

This manual is designed to be a practical reference that you can use at any time. Each chapter is self-contained, allowing you to focus on specific areas of interest or concern. You can read through the entire manual to gain a broad understanding of disaster preparedness, or refer to individual chapters as needed based on the type of disaster you are facing.

Your Role in Disaster Preparedness

Ultimately, disaster preparedness is a personal responsibility that requires commitment and proactive effort. By taking the time to read this manual and implement the strategies outlined within, you are investing in your own safety and well-being. Remember, preparedness is not a one-time task but an ongoing process that involves continual learning and adaptation.

Chapter 01
Preparing for Natural Disasters

Understanding Different Types of Natural Disasters

- **Earthquakes**:Explanation of tectonic movements, fault lines, and regions most susceptible to earthquakes. Discuss the unpredictability of earthquakes and the importance of seismic monitoring.
- **Floods**: Differentiate between flash floods, river floods, and coastal flooding. Explain the factors contributing to floods, such as heavy rainfall, storm surges, and snowmelt.
- **Hurricanes and Typhoons**:Detail the formation of tropical storms, the role of warm ocean waters, and the classification of hurricanes and typhoons. Discuss how climate change is affecting storm intensity.
- **Wildfires**: Discuss the causes of wildfires, including natural factors like lightning and human activities such as arson. Explain the role of drought and high winds in wildfire spread.
- **Tornadoes**:Describe the formation of tornadoes, the role of supercells, and the regions most at risk, such as Tornado Alley in the United States.

Building a Disaster Survival Kit

- **Essential Items**: A detailed list of must-have items including water, non-perishable food, first aid supplies, flashlights, batteries, and emergency communication devices.

- **Customizing Your Kit**: Tips for tailoring your kit based on specific disaster risks (e.g., waterproof bags for flood-prone areas, dust masks for wildfire-prone regions).
- **Long-Term Storage and Maintenance**: How to store your kit properly to ensure items remain usable, and tips for regularly checking and updating supplies.

Creating a Family Emergency Plan

Communication Strategies: How to establish communication channels among family members, including the use of out-of-area contacts and social media.

- **Designating Meeting Points**: The importance of having both a local and an out-of-town meeting place in case of evacuation.
- **Practice Drills**: The value of regularly practicing your emergency plan with all family members to ensure everyone knows what to do.

Home Safety Preparations

- **Securing Your Home**: How to fortify your home against different types of disasters (e.g., securing heavy furniture for earthquakes, installing storm shutters for hurricanes).
- **Safe Zones**: Identifying the safest areas in your home during specific disasters, such as

basements for tornadoes or interior rooms for hurricanes.

- **Utility Management**: Preparing for potential utility failures by learning how to shut off gas, electricity, and water to prevent further damage.

Community and Government Resources

- **Local Emergency Services**: How to access and utilize local emergency services, shelters, and relief centers.
- **Staying Informed**: The importance of signing up for local alerts, understanding warning systems, and using reliable news sources.
- **Community Preparedness**: Tips for working with neighbors to create a community emergency plan, pooling resources, and supporting each other during a disaster.

Evacuation Planning

- **When to Evacuate**: Understanding evacuation orders and knowing when it's time to leave. Discuss the risks of staying behind and the importance of early evacuation.
- **Creating an Evacuation Checklist**: A comprehensive list of what to take with you, including vital documents, medications, and emergency supplies.

- **Evacuating with Pets and Vulnerable Family Members**:Special considerations for evacuating with pets, elderly relatives, or those with disabilities. Tips on finding pet-friendly shelters and ensuring everyone's needs are met.

Chapter 02
Surviving Wildfires

Understanding Wildfire Risks

- **Causes of Wildfires**: Natural causes like lightning and human-induced factors such as arson, campfires, and power lines. Explanation of how drought and high winds exacerbate wildfire risks.
- **High-Risk Areas**: Identification of regions most vulnerable to wildfires, such as California, Australia, and Mediterranean countries. Discussion of the "wildland-urban interface" where human habitation meets wilderness.
- **Climate Change and Wildfires**: How climate change is increasing the frequency and intensity of wildfires, and what this means for future preparedness efforts.

Wildfire Preparedness

- **Creating a Defensible Space**: Steps to create a defensible space around your home to reduce wildfire risks, including clearing vegetation, removing flammable materials, and using fire-resistant landscaping.
- **Home Hardening Techniques**: How to make your home more fire-resistant, including using fire-resistant building materials, installing ember-resistant vents, and maintaining a fire-safe roof.

- **Emergency Kit and Evacuation Plan**: What to include in a wildfire-specific emergency kit, such as respirators, goggles, and fire blankets.

Tips for developing a quick evacuation plan

During a Wildfire

- **Evacuation Orders**: Understanding different levels of evacuation orders and when to leave. The importance of leaving early to avoid being trapped by the fire.
- **Sheltering in Place**: When and how to safely shelter in place during a wildfire. Precautions to take, such as sealing your home against smoke and having a safe room.
- **Dealing with Smoke and Air Quality**: Tips for protecting yourself from smoke inhalation, including using air purifiers, wearing masks, and avoiding outdoor activities during poor air quality days.

Post-Wildfire Recovery

- **Returning Home Safely**: How to safely return home after a wildfire, including checking for structural damage, gas leaks, and remaining hot spots.
- **Cleaning Up Safely**: Steps to take when cleaning up after a wildfire, such as wearing

protective gear, handling ash and debris carefully, and avoiding contaminated areas.

- **Health and Mental Well-Being**: Addressing the psychological effects of surviving a wildfire, including stress, anxiety, and trauma. Tips for seeking professional help and rebuilding your life.

Long-Term Wildfire Preparedness

- **Rebuilding After a Wildfire**: How to rebuild your home and community after a wildfire, with a focus on fire-resistant materials and designs. The importance of planning for future wildfire risks.
- **Community Wildfire Preparedness Programs**: How to participate in local wildfire preparedness efforts, including community fire breaks, evacuation planning, and public education.
- **Insurance and Financial Planning**: Understanding wildfire insurance, how to file claims, and financial planning for rebuilding and recovery.

Staying Informed and Ready

- **Monitoring Wildfire Risks**: The importance of staying updated on wildfire risks, weather conditions, and local fire warnings. How to use technology and apps to monitor fires.

- **Regular Drills and Community Engagement**: Conducting regular wildfire drills at home and participating in community preparedness events. Tips for staying engaged and informed.

Adapting to Changing Risks: Recognizing the evolving nature of wildfire risks due to climate change and adapting your preparedness plans accordingly.

Chapter 03
Surviving Winter Storms and Extreme Cold

Understanding Winter Storms

- **Types of Winter Storms**: Explanation of different types of winter storms, including blizzards, ice storms, and snow squalls. Discuss the conditions that lead to each and their potential impacts.
- **Extreme Cold and Its Dangers**: The risks associated with extreme cold, including hypothermia, frostbite, and the dangers of prolonged exposure to freezing temperatures.
- **Climate Change and Winter Weather**: How climate change is affecting winter storm patterns, with some regions experiencing more severe and unpredictable winter weather.

Winter Storm Preparedness

- **Home Insulation and Heating**: How to prepare your home for winter storms, including proper insulation, heating systems, and emergency backup heat sources.
- **Winter Survival Kit**: Essential items for a winter-specific emergency kit, such as warm clothing, blankets, non-perishable food, and water.
- **Vehicle Preparedness**: Preparing your vehicle for winter weather, including snow tires, chains, emergency kits, and understanding the dangers of driving in icy conditions.

During a Winter Storm

- **Sheltering in Place**: How to stay safe and warm during a winter storm, including the importance of staying indoors, conserving heat, and using safe heating methods.
- **Dealing with Power Outages**: Strategies for coping with power outages during extreme cold, including the use of generators, conserving fuel, and staying warm without electricity.
- **Avoiding Hypothermia and Frostbite**: Tips for recognizing the signs of hypothermia and frostbite and how to prevent these conditions during extreme cold weather.

Post-Winter Storm Recovery

- **Assessing Damage and Ensuring Safety**: How to safely assess your home and property after a winter storm, including checking for ice dams, burst pipes, and structural damage.
- **Clearing Snow and Ice Safely**: Tips for clearing snow and ice from walkways, driveways, and roofs without causing injury or further damage.
- **Health and Well-Being**: Addressing the physical and psychological impact of surviving a severe winter storm, including dealing with isolation, stress, and cold-related illnesses.

Long-Term Winter Storm Preparedness

- **Improving Home Resilience**: How to make your home more resilient to winter storms, including upgrading insulation, installing storm windows, and ensuring backup heat sources.
- **Community Winter Preparedness Programs**: How to participate in local winter preparedness efforts, including community snow removal, emergency shelters, and public education.
- **Insurance and Financial Planning**: Understanding winter storm insurance, what it covers, and how to plan financially for winter-related damage and recovery.

Staying Informed and Ready

- **Monitoring Weather Conditions**: The importance of staying updated on weather forecasts, winter storm warnings, and extreme cold alerts. How to use technology and apps to stay informed.
- **Regular Drills and Preparedness Updates**: Conducting regular winter storm drills and updating your preparedness plan annually. Tips for staying engaged with local emergency services and community efforts.

Adapting to Changing Risks: Recognizing the evolving nature of winter storm risks due to climate change and adjusting your preparedness plans accordingly.

Chapter 04
Surviving Heatwaves and Extreme Heat

Understanding Heatwaves

- **Causes and Risks of Heatwaves**: Explanation of how heatwaves form, including high-pressure systems and the effects of urban heat islands. Discuss the health risks associated with extreme heat, such as heatstroke and dehydration.
- **Vulnerable Populations**: Identification of groups most at risk during heatwaves, including the elderly, children, and those with pre-existing health conditions. Discuss the importance of community support for vulnerable individuals.
- **Climate Change and Rising Temperatures**: How climate change is contributing to more frequent and severe heatwaves, and what this means for future preparedness efforts.

Heatwave Preparedness

- **Home Cooling Techniques**: Tips for keeping your home cool during a heatwave, including the use of fans, air conditioning, and shading windows. How to reduce heat buildup and maintain a comfortable indoor temperature.
- **Staying Hydrated and Healthy**: The importance of staying hydrated during extreme heat, including tips for drinking enough water, avoiding alcohol and caffeine, and recognizing the signs of heat-related illnesses.

- **Heatwave Survival Kit**: Essential items for a heatwave-specific emergency kit, such as water, cooling towels, sunscreen, and lightweight, breathable clothing.

During a Heatwave

- **Staying Cool Indoors**: How to stay cool indoors during a heatwave, including the use of air conditioning, fans, and cool showers. Tips for avoiding strenuous activities and staying in the coolest parts of your home.
- **Protecting Yourself Outdoors**: Strategies for staying safe if you need to be outside during a heatwave, including wearing protective clothing, using sunscreen, and taking frequent breaks in the shade.
- **Helping Vulnerable Individuals**: How to assist vulnerable individuals during a heatwave, such as checking on elderly neighbors, providing access to cooling centers, and ensuring children and pets stay cool.

Post-Heatwave Recovery

- **Health Monitoring**: Tips for monitoring your health and the health of others after a heatwave, including recognizing delayed symptoms of heat-related illnesses.
- **Assessing Heat Damage**: How to assess and address any heat-related damage to your home,

such as warped wood, damaged electronics, or dead landscaping.

- **Rehydration and Recovery**: The importance of rehydration and rest after a heatwave, including tips for replenishing electrolytes and recovering from heat exhaustion.

Long-Term Heatwave Preparedness

- **Improving Home Cooling Efficiency**: How to improve your home's cooling efficiency, including upgrading insulation, installing energy-efficient windows, and using reflective roofing materials.
- **Community Heatwave Preparedness Programs**: How to participate in local heatwave preparedness efforts, including cooling center initiatives, public education, and support for vulnerable populations.
- **Insurance and Financial Planning**: Understanding insurance coverage for heat-related damage, what it covers, and how to plan financially for future heatwaves.

Staying Informed and Ready

- **Monitoring Weather Conditions**: The importance of staying updated on weather forecasts, heatwave warnings, and extreme heat alerts. How to use technology and apps to stay informed.

- **Regular Drills and Preparedness Updates**: Conducting regular heatwave drills and updating your preparedness plan annually. Tips for staying engaged with local emergency services and community efforts.
- **Adapting to Changing Risks**: Recognizing the evolving nature of heatwave risks due to climate change and adjusting your preparedness plans accordingly.

Chapter 05
Surviving Droughts

Understanding Droughts

- **Causes of Droughts**: Explanation of the meteorological, hydrological, and agricultural factors that contribute to droughts. Discuss the role of climate patterns like El Niño and La Niña.
- **Impact of Droughts on Society**: The wide-ranging effects of droughts on agriculture, water supply, and economies. How droughts can lead to food shortages, water rationing, and increased wildfire risks.
- **Climate Change and Droughts**: How climate change is exacerbating drought conditions in many regions, leading to longer and more severe droughts. The implications for global water resources.

Drought Preparedness

- **Water Conservation Techniques**: Tips for conserving water during a drought, including fixing leaks, using water-efficient appliances, and implementing greywater systems.
- **Drought-Resistant Landscaping**: How to design and maintain a drought-resistant garden, including choosing native plants, using mulch, and implementing drip irrigation.
- **Building a Water Reserve**: Strategies for building a water reserve during non-drought

times, including rainwater harvesting, using cisterns, and water storage guidelines.

During a Drought

- **Prioritizing Water Usage**: How to prioritize water usage during a drought, including strategies for rationing water and ensuring essential needs are met first.
- **Health and Hygiene**: Maintaining health and hygiene with limited water supply, including tips for efficient bathing, handwashing, and sanitation.
- **Supporting Agriculture**: How to support local agriculture during a drought, including buying from drought-resistant farms, supporting water-efficient practices, and understanding the challenges farmers face.

Post-Drought Recovery

- **Replenishing Water Supplies**: Strategies for replenishing water supplies after a drought, including recharging groundwater, managing reservoirs, and restoring ecosystems.
- **Soil Recovery and Erosion Control**: Tips for helping soil recover after a drought, including erosion control, soil conditioning, and planting cover crops.
- **Community and Economic Recovery**: How communities can recover from a drought,

including rebuilding local economies, addressing water infrastructure, and planning for future droughts.

Long-Term Drought Preparedness

- **Sustainable Water Management**: The importance of sustainable water management practices, including efficient irrigation, water recycling, and protecting natural water sources.
- **Community Drought Preparedness Programs**: How to participate in local drought preparedness efforts, including public education, water conservation initiatives, and drought planning.
- **Insurance and Financial Planning**: Understanding insurance coverage for drought-related losses, what it covers, and how to plan financially for future droughts.

Staying Informed and Ready

- **Monitoring Drought Conditions**: The importance of staying updated on drought conditions, water restrictions, and conservation efforts. How to use technology and apps to stay informed.
- **Regular Drills and Preparedness Updates**: Conducting regular drought drills and updating your preparedness plan annually.

Tips for staying engaged with local emergency services and community efforts.

● **Adapting to Changing Risks**: Recognizing the evolving nature of drought risks due to climate change and adjusting your preparedness plans accordingly.

Chapter 06

Surviving Earthquakes

Understanding Earthquakes

- **Causes of Earthquakes**: Explanation of tectonic plate movements, fault lines, and seismic activity. Discuss the different types of earthquakes and their potential impacts.
- **Earthquake-Prone Regions**: Identification of regions most susceptible to earthquakes, including the Pacific Ring of Fire, California, Japan, and other high-risk areas.
- **Earthquake Magnitude and Intensity**: Overview of the Richter scale and the Modified Mercalli Intensity scale used to measure the magnitude and intensity of earthquakes. How these scales help in understanding the potential impact of an earthquake.

Earthquake Preparedness

- **Building Earthquake-Resistant Structures**: How to design and retrofit buildings to withstand earthquakes, including using base isolators, shear walls, and flexible building materials.
- **Creating an Earthquake Emergency Kit**: Essential items for an earthquake-specific emergency kit, such as first aid supplies, water, non-perishable food, and sturdy shoes.
- **Developing an Earthquake Response Plan**: Steps to create a family or workplace earthquake response plan, including

identifying safe spots, practicing "Drop, Cover, and Hold On," and establishing communication strategies.

During an Earthquake

- **Immediate Actions**: What to do when an earthquake strikes, including the "Drop, Cover, and Hold On" technique, and staying away from windows, heavy furniture, and other hazards.
- **Sheltering in Different Locations**: Specific actions to take depending on your location during an earthquake, such as being indoors, in a high-rise building, or outdoors.
- **Evacuating After an Earthquake**: When and how to evacuate safely after an earthquake, including understanding aftershocks, checking for damage, and avoiding downed power lines and gas leaks.

Post-Earthquake Recovery

- **Assessing Damage and Ensuring Safety**: How to safely assess your home and surroundings after an earthquake, including checking for structural damage, gas leaks, and potential landslides.
- **First Aid and Emergency Response**: Providing first aid to injured individuals and knowing

when to call for emergency services. Tips for dealing with shock and trauma.

- **Dealing with Insurance Claims**: Understanding the process of filing insurance claims after an earthquake, including documenting damage, working with adjusters, and knowing your coverage.

Long-Term Earthquake Preparedness

- **Retrofitting Buildings**: The importance of retrofitting older buildings to meet modern earthquake-resistant standards. Discuss the costs and benefits of retrofitting and available financial assistance.
- **Community Earthquake Preparedness Programs**: How to participate in local earthquake preparedness efforts, including public education, earthquake drills, and building code enforcement.
- **Insurance and Financial Planning**: Understanding earthquake insurance, what it covers, and how to plan financially for rebuilding and recovery after an earthquake.

Staying Informed and Ready

- **Monitoring Seismic Activity**: The importance of staying updated on seismic activity, earthquake warnings, and aftershock predictions. How to use technology and apps to stay informed.

- **Regular Drills and Preparedness Updates**: Conducting regular earthquake drills and updating your preparedness plan annually. Tips for staying engaged with local emergency services and community efforts.
- **Adapting to Changing Risks**: Recognizing the evolving nature of earthquake risks due to urban development and climate change, and adjusting your preparedness plans accordingly.

Chapter 07
Surviving Floods and Flash Floods

Understanding Floods

- **Types of Floods**: Explanation of different types of floods, including river floods, flash floods, coastal floods, and urban floods. Discuss the causes and potential impacts of each type of flood.
- **Flood-Prone Areas**: Identification of regions most susceptible to floods, including low-lying areas, riverbanks, coastal regions, and areas with poor drainage systems. Discuss the increasing risk of floods in urban areas due to climate change and infrastructure challenges.
- **Climate Change and Flooding**: How climate change is contributing to more frequent and severe flooding events, including sea-level rise, increased rainfall, and extreme weather patterns.

Types of Floods and Their Causes

- **Flash Floods**: Rapid flooding caused by intense rainfall over a short period. How to identify flash flood-prone areas and the dangers they pose.
- **River Flooding**: Causes of river flooding, including snowmelt, prolonged rainfall, and dam failure. How to monitor river levels and recognize early warning signs.
- **Coastal Flooding**: The impact of storm surges, tsunamis, and rising sea levels on coastal areas.

How to prepare for and respond to coastal floods.

- **Urban Flooding**: Causes of flooding in cities, including poor drainage systems and impermeable surfaces. How to protect yourself in an urban flood situation.

Flood Preparedness

- **Flood-Proofing Your Home**: Strategies for flood-proofing your home, including installing sump pumps, sealing basements, elevating utilities, and using water-resistant building materials.
- **Creating a Flood Emergency Kit**: Essential items for a flood-specific emergency kit, such as waterproof bags for important documents, flashlights, first aid supplies, and life jackets.
- **Developing a Flood Evacuation Plan**: Steps to create a family or community flood evacuation plan, including identifying evacuation routes, establishing communication plans, and knowing how to shut off utilities.

During a Flood

- **Evacuating Safely**: When and how to evacuate safely during a flood, including tips for avoiding flooded roads, staying informed of flood warnings, and knowing where to seek shelter.

- **Sheltering in Place**: What to do if evacuation is not possible, including how to shelter in place safely, moving to higher floors, and avoiding contact with floodwaters.
- **Protecting Yourself Outdoors**: If caught outside during a flood, how to find a safe location, avoid fast-moving water, and signal for help. Tips for using flotation devices and staying above water.

Post-Flood Recovery

- **Returning Home Safely**: How to safely return home after a flood, including checking for hidden dangers like structural damage, mold, and contaminated water. Tips for re-entering your home and assessing damage.
- **Dealing with Water Damage**: How to clean up and repair water damage, including drying out your home, removing contaminated materials, and preventing mold growth.
- **Health and Safety Considerations**: Addressing health and safety concerns after a flood, including dealing with contaminated water, food safety, and managing stress and trauma.

Long-Term Flood Preparedness

- **Improving Flood Resilience**: How to make your home and community more resilient to future floods, including upgrading infrastructure, implementing flood barriers, and improving drainage systems.

- **Community Flood Preparedness Programs**: How to participate in local flood preparedness efforts, including public education, floodplain management, and emergency response planning.
- **Insurance and Financial Planning**: Understanding flood insurance, what it covers, and how to plan financially for rebuilding and recovery after a flood.

Staying Informed and Ready

- **Monitoring Flood Conditions**: The importance of staying updated on flood warnings, weather forecasts, and evacuation orders. How to use technology and apps to stay informed.
- **Regular Drills and Preparedness Updates**: Conducting regular flood drills and updating your preparedness plan annually. Tips for staying engaged with local emergency services and community efforts.
- **Adapting to Changing Risks**: Recognizing the evolving nature of flood risks due to climate change, urban development, and changing weather patterns. Adjusting your preparedness plans accordingly.

Chapter 08
Surviving Tsunamis

Understanding Tsunamis

- **Causes of Tsunamis**: Explanation of the primary causes of tsunamis, including undersea earthquakes, volcanic eruptions, and landslides. Discuss the role of tectonic plate movements and the potential for tsunamis in different regions.
- **Tsunami-Prone Areas**: Identification of regions most susceptible to tsunamis, including coastal areas along the Pacific Ocean, the Indian Ocean, and the Mediterranean Sea. Discuss the importance of recognizing tsunami warning signs in these areas.
- **Tsunami Behavior and Impact**: How tsunamis form and travel across oceans, including the speed, height, and impact of tsunami waves. Explanation of the different stages of a tsunami and their potential effects on coastal communities.

Tsunami Preparedness

- **Creating a Tsunami Evacuation Plan**: Steps to create a family or community tsunami evacuation plan, including identifying high ground, establishing communication plans, and practicing evacuation drills.
- **Tsunami Warning Systems**: Understanding how tsunami warning systems work, including the role of seismic sensors, buoys, and public

alert systems. Tips for staying informed and responding quickly to warnings.

- **Preparing Your Home for a Tsunami**: Strategies for preparing your home for a potential tsunami, including securing heavy furniture, moving valuable items to higher ground, and understanding flood zones.

During a Tsunami

- **Evacuating Safely**: When and how to evacuate safely during a tsunami warning, including tips for reaching high ground, avoiding low-lying areas, and staying informed of tsunami progress.
- **Sheltering in Place**: What to do if evacuation is not possible, including how to shelter in place safely, moving to the highest level of a sturdy building, and avoiding contact with tsunami waters.
- **Protecting Yourself Outdoors**: If caught outside during a tsunami, how to find a safe location, avoid fast-moving water, and signal for help. Tips for using flotation devices and staying above water.

Post-Tsunami Recovery

- **Returning Home Safely**: How to safely return home after a tsunami, including checking for hidden dangers like structural damage, contaminated water, and debris. Tips for re-entering your home and assessing damage.

- **Dealing with Water and Debris**: How to clean up and repair water damage and debris, including drying out your home, removing contaminated materials, and preventing mold growth.
- **Health and Safety Considerations**: Addressing health and safety concerns after a tsunami, including dealing with contaminated water, food safety, and managing stress and trauma.

Long-Term Tsunami Preparedness

- **Improving Coastal Resilience**: How to make coastal communities more resilient to future tsunamis, including upgrading infrastructure, implementing early warning systems, and improving evacuation routes.
- **Community Tsunami Preparedness Programs**: How to participate in local tsunami preparedness efforts, including public education, tsunami drills, and emergency response planning.
- **Insurance and Financial Planning**: Understanding tsunami insurance, what it covers, and how to plan financially for rebuilding and recovery after a tsunami.

Staying Informed and Ready

- **Monitoring Tsunami Conditions**: The importance of staying updated on tsunami warnings, seismic activity, and evacuation orders. How to use technology and apps to stay informed.
- **Regular Drills and Preparedness Updates**: Conducting regular tsunami drills and updating your preparedness plan annually. Tips for staying engaged with local emergency services and community efforts.
- **Adapting to Changing Risks**: Recognizing the evolving nature of tsunami risks due to seismic activity, climate change, and coastal development. Adjusting your preparedness plans accordingly.

Chapter 09
Surviving Landslides and Mudflows

Understanding Landslides and Mudflows

- **Causes of Landslides**: Explanation of the primary causes of landslides, including natural factors like heavy rainfall, earthquakes, volcanic activity, and human activities such as deforestation, mining, and construction. Discuss how slope stability, soil composition, and water saturation influence the likelihood of a landslide.

- **Types of Landslides and Mudflows**: Overview of different types of landslides, including rockfalls, debris flows, and earth slides, as well as mudflows, which are rapid movements of water-saturated earth materials. Discuss the characteristics and impact of each type.

- **Landslide-Prone Areas**: Identification of regions most susceptible to landslides and mudflows, including mountainous areas, steep slopes, and regions with a history of heavy rainfall or seismic activity. Discuss the importance of understanding local geology and terrain.

Landslide and Mudflow Preparedness

- **Recognizing Warning Signs**: How to recognize early warning signs of landslides and mudflows, including unusual sounds like rumbling, ground movement, cracks in the ground, and changes in water flow. Tips for monitoring local weather and staying alert to environmental changes.

- **Preparing Your Home**: Strategies for reducing landslide risk around your home, including proper drainage management, retaining walls, and avoiding construction on unstable slopes. Discuss the importance of regular inspections and maintenance to ensure slope stability.
- **Developing an Evacuation Plan**: Steps to create a family or community evacuation plan for landslides, including identifying safe routes, establishing communication plans, and practicing evacuation drills. Emphasize the need for quick action and awareness of local hazards.

During a Landslide or Mudflow

- **Evacuating Safely**: When and how to evacuate safely during a landslide or mudflow, including tips for recognizing immediate dangers, avoiding river valleys and low-lying areas, and moving to higher ground. Discuss the importance of heeding evacuation orders and staying away from affected areas.
- **Sheltering in Place**: What to do if evacuation is not possible, including how to shelter in place safely, identifying safe areas within your home, and protecting yourself from debris and falling objects. Tips for communicating your location to emergency services.

- **Protecting Yourself Outdoors**: If caught outside during a landslide or mudflow, how to find a safe location, avoid fast-moving debris, and signal for help. Discuss the importance of staying aware of your surroundings and moving away from hazardous areas.

Post-Landslide and Mudflow Recovery

- **Returning Home Safely**: How to safely return home after a landslide or mudflow, including checking for hidden dangers like structural damage, unstable ground, and blocked roads. Tips for re-entering your home and assessing damage.
- **Dealing with Debris and Damage**: How to clean up and repair damage caused by landslides and mudflows, including removing debris, stabilizing slopes, and repairing damaged infrastructure. Discuss the importance of professional assessments for serious damage.
- **Health and Safety Considerations**: Addressing health and safety concerns after a landslide or mudflow, including dealing with contaminated water, food safety, and managing stress and trauma. Discuss the potential for further landslides and how to stay prepared.

Long-Term Landslide and Mudflow Preparedness

- **Improving Community Resilience**: How to make your community more resilient to future landslides and mudflows, including implementing early warning systems, improving land-use planning, and promoting public education on landslide risks. Discuss the importance of collaboration between local authorities, residents, and experts.
- **Participating in Landslide Mitigation Programs**: How to get involved in local landslide mitigation efforts, including reforestation projects, slope stabilization initiatives, and disaster preparedness workshops. Discuss the benefits of community engagement in reducing landslide risks.
- **Insurance and Financial Planning**: Understanding landslide insurance, what it covers, and how to plan financially for rebuilding and recovery after a landslide or mudflow. Discuss the challenges of securing coverage and the importance of proactive risk management.

Staying Informed and Ready

- **Monitoring Landslide Conditions**: The importance of staying updated on weather forecasts, soil saturation levels, and local landslide warnings. How to use technology, such as apps and alert systems, to stay informed.

- **Regular Drills and Preparedness Updates**: Conducting regular landslide drills and updating your preparedness plan annually. Tips for staying engaged with local emergency services, geological surveys, and community efforts.

- **Adapting to Changing Risks**: Recognizing the evolving nature of landslide risks due to climate change, deforestation, and urban development. Adjusting your preparedness plans accordingly, including considering relocation if necessary.

Chapter 10
Surviving Volcanic Eruptions

Understanding Volcanic Eruptions

- **Types of Volcanic Eruptions**: Explanation of different types of volcanic eruptions, including explosive eruptions, effusive eruptions, and phreatomagmatic eruptions. Discuss how each type affects the environment and human safety.
- **Volcano Structure and Behavior**: Overview of the anatomy of a volcano, including the magma chamber, vent, crater, and lava flow. Describe how volcanic activity, such as lava flows, ash clouds, pyroclastic flows, and lahars, impacts surrounding areas.
- **Volcanic Hazards**: Identification of various hazards associated with volcanic eruptions, including ashfall, lava flows, pyroclastic surges, volcanic gases, and lahars. Explain the immediate and long-term effects of these hazards on health, property, and the environment.

Volcanic Eruption Preparedness

- **Recognizing Volcano Warning Signs**: How to recognize early warning signs of volcanic activity, such as increased seismic activity, ground deformation, gas emissions, and changes in volcanic plume behavior. Discuss the importance of staying informed through geological monitoring services.

- **Emergency Kit and Supplies**: What to include in a volcanic eruption emergency kit, including masks or respirators to protect against ash inhalation, first aid supplies, non-perishable food, water, and personal documents. Emphasize the need for adequate protection against ash and volcanic gases.
- **Evacuation Planning**: Steps to create a family or community evacuation plan, including identifying safe evacuation routes, establishing meeting points, and knowing where to go for shelter. Discuss the importance of following evacuation orders and staying informed about evacuation procedures.

During a Volcanic Eruption

- **Immediate Actions**: What to do during a volcanic eruption, including seeking shelter indoors, sealing windows and doors to prevent ash from entering, and avoiding unnecessary outdoor activities. Tips for staying updated with official information and warnings.
- **Protecting Your Health**: How to protect yourself from volcanic ash and gases, including using masks or respirators, keeping indoor air clean, and minimizing physical exertion. Discuss the importance of monitoring air quality and taking precautions to avoid respiratory issues.

- **Handling Lava Flows and Pyroclastic Flows**: What to do if lava flows or pyroclastic flows are approaching, including evacuating to higher ground, avoiding areas with visible lava or pyroclastic surges, and staying away from the flow path. Discuss the speed and unpredictability of these hazards.

Post-Eruption Recovery

- **Returning Home Safely**: How to safely return home after a volcanic eruption, including checking for structural damage, assessing the impact of ashfall, and dealing with potential gas leaks. Tips for assessing the safety of your home and property before re-entry.
- **Cleaning Up Ash and Debris**: How to clean volcanic ash and debris from your property, including using proper protective gear, avoiding sweeping or vacuuming fine ash particles, and following local guidelines for ash disposal. Discuss the importance of thorough cleanup to prevent long-term damage.
- **Health and Environmental Concerns**: Addressing health concerns related to ash inhalation, exposure to volcanic gases, and contaminated water sources. Discuss long-term environmental impacts, such as soil fertility issues and water contamination, and how to address these problems.

Long-Term Volcanic Eruption Preparedness

- **Volcano Monitoring and Alerts**: How to stay informed about ongoing volcanic activity, including subscribing to volcano alert systems, following updates from geological agencies, and participating in community preparedness programs. Emphasize the importance of staying vigilant and updated.
- **Community Resilience and Support**: Building community resilience to volcanic eruptions through local disaster preparedness programs, community drills, and support networks. Discuss the role of community organizations and local government in disaster response and recovery.
- **Insurance and Financial Recovery**: Understanding volcanic eruption insurance, what it covers, and how to manage financial recovery after an eruption. Discuss the importance of documenting damage, working with insurance companies, and seeking financial assistance if needed.

Staying Prepared and Informed

- **Regular Drills and Preparedness Reviews**: Conducting regular volcanic eruption drills and reviewing your preparedness plan annually. Tips for staying engaged with local emergency services, geological surveys, and community preparedness efforts.

- **Adapting to Evolving Risks**: Recognizing how volcanic risks may change due to new volcanic activity, environmental changes, or shifts in geological conditions. Adjusting your preparedness plan and staying informed about evolving risks.
- **Educational Resources and Community Involvement**: Utilizing educational resources on volcanic hazards and getting involved in community preparedness initiatives. Discuss the benefits of ongoing education and community engagement in enhancing disaster resilience.

Chapter 11
Surviving Severe Storms and Tornadoes

Understanding Severe Storms and Tornadoes

- **Types of Severe Storms**: Overview of different types of severe storms, including thunderstorms, hailstorms, and tornadoes. Discuss their characteristics, formation processes, and the damage they can cause.
- **Tornado Formation and Classification**: Explanation of how tornadoes form, their classification based on intensity (EF-0 to EF-5), and the scale used to measure their strength. Discuss tornado patterns, common occurrences, and geographic regions prone to tornadoes.
- **Storm and Tornado Risks**: Identification of the risks associated with severe storms and tornadoes, including wind damage, flooding, hail, and flying debris. Discuss the potential impacts on infrastructure, property, and human safety.

Preparedness for Severe Storms and Tornadoes

- **Emergency Kit and Supplies**: Essentials for an emergency kit to prepare for severe storms and tornadoes, including weather radios, first aid supplies, non-perishable food, and water. Emphasize the importance of having a ready-to-go kit for quick evacuation or sheltering.
- **Creating a Family Emergency Plan**: How to develop a comprehensive family emergency plan, including designated meeting places,

communication strategies, and roles and responsibilities. Discuss the importance of regular drills and updating the plan as needed.

- **Building and Home Safety**: Tips for securing your home and property against severe storms and tornadoes, such as reinforcing windows, securing outdoor items, and installing a storm shelter or safe room. Discuss structural improvements to enhance home resilience.

During Severe Storms and Tornadoes

- **Seeking Shelter**: Guidelines for finding and utilizing safe shelters during severe storms and tornadoes, including basement shelters, interior rooms, and designated storm shelters. Discuss the best practices for sheltering to ensure safety.
- **Emergency Communication**: Strategies for staying informed during severe weather events, including using weather radios, mobile apps, and emergency alerts. Discuss the importance of receiving timely information and following official guidance.
- **Safety Practices and Precautions**: Actions to take during severe storms and tornadoes to ensure personal safety, such as avoiding windows, staying low to the ground, and protecting your head. Discuss how to manage and mitigate immediate risks.

Health and Safety Measures

Handling Injuries and Medical Emergencies: How to manage injuries and medical emergencies resulting from severe storms and tornadoes, including first aid for cuts, bruises, and broken bones. Discuss when to seek professional medical help and available resources.

- **Addressing Mental Health Impact**: Recognizing and addressing the mental health impact of severe weather events, including stress, anxiety, and trauma. Discuss coping strategies and available mental health support services.
- **Dealing with Property Damage**: Steps to assess and address property damage, including documenting damages, contacting insurance providers, and arranging for repairs. Discuss how to prioritize repairs and safety checks.

Post-Storm Recovery

- **Assessing and Reporting Damage**: How to assess and report damage to property, utilities, and infrastructure after a severe storm or tornado. Discuss the importance of documenting damage for insurance claims and recovery assistance.
- **Restoring Normalcy**: Tips for restoring normalcy and routine after a severe weather

event, including cleaning up debris, repairing damaged property, and resuming daily activities. Discuss the importance of gradual recovery and support systems.

- **Community Support and Resources**: Utilizing community resources and support networks for recovery and rebuilding efforts. Discuss the role of local organizations, disaster relief agencies, and community initiatives in aiding recovery.

Long-Term Preparedness

- **Improving Home Resilience**: Strategies for enhancing home resilience to future severe storms and tornadoes, such as retrofitting structures, installing impact-resistant windows, and creating defensible space around the property. Discuss long-term investments in home safety.
- **Advocacy for Disaster Preparedness**: Engaging in advocacy for policies and initiatives that improve community preparedness for severe weather events. Discuss how to support local and national efforts to enhance disaster resilience and response.
- **Educational Resources and Outreach**: Utilizing educational resources to stay informed about severe weather safety and participating in outreach programs to raise

awareness. Discuss the value of ongoing education and community engagement in preparedness.

Staying Informed and Engaged

- **Monitoring Weather Alerts and Warnings**: How to stay informed about weather alerts and warnings, including subscribing to weather notifications, using weather apps, and following local news updates. Emphasize the importance of staying updated on weather conditions.
- **Participating in Storm Safety Programs**: Engaging in storm safety programs and initiatives to improve personal and community preparedness. Discuss the benefits of participating in educational programs and public safety campaigns focused on severe weather.
- **Sharing Knowledge and Resources**: Sharing knowledge and resources about severe weather safety with others, including family, friends, and neighbors. Discuss how community collaboration and information sharing can enhance overall preparedness and response.

Chapter 12
Navigating Economic Disasters

Understanding Economic Disasters

- **Types of Economic Disasters**: Overview of various economic disasters, including financial crises, recessions, and depressions. Discuss their causes, impacts, and how they affect individuals, businesses, and economies.
- **Indicators of Economic Downturn**: Key indicators that signal an impending economic disaster, such as rising unemployment rates, declining GDP, and falling stock markets. Explain how these indicators can be monitored and interpreted.
- **Historical Examples**: Examination of historical economic disasters, including the Great Depression, the 2008 financial crisis, and hyperinflation in various countries. Discuss the lessons learned from these events and their relevance to current economic conditions.

Preparing for Economic Disasters

- **Personal Financial Planning**: Strategies for personal financial planning to withstand economic downturns, including budgeting, saving, and investing. Discuss how to create a financial safety net and prioritize essential expenses.
- **Debt Management**: Tips for managing and reducing debt to improve financial stability during economic crises. Discuss strategies for

consolidating debt, negotiating with creditors, and avoiding high-interest loans.

- **Emergency Savings Fund**: Importance of building and maintaining an emergency savings fund to cover unexpected expenses during economic downturns. Provide guidelines for determining the appropriate amount and ways to build this fund.

During Economic Disasters

- **Adjusting to Financial Challenges**: Practical steps for adjusting to financial challenges during an economic disaster, including reducing discretionary spending, finding additional sources of income, and making temporary lifestyle changes.
- **Accessing Assistance Programs**: Information on various assistance programs and resources available during economic crises, including unemployment benefits, food assistance, and emergency loans. Provide guidance on how to apply for and utilize these resources.
- **Protecting Assets**: Strategies for protecting personal and business assets during economic downturns, including insurance, diversification, and safeguarding investments. Discuss how to mitigate risks and avoid financial losses.

Business Continuity Planning

- **Creating a Business Continuity Plan**: Steps for developing a business continuity plan to ensure that operations can continue during economic disruptions. Discuss key components such as risk assessment, contingency planning, and communication strategies.
- **Managing Cash Flow**: Techniques for managing cash flow effectively during economic downturns, including forecasting, expense control, and revenue optimization. Discuss the importance of maintaining liquidity and financial flexibility.
- **Employee and Stakeholder Communication**: Best practices for communicating with employees, customers, and other stakeholders during economic crises. Discuss how to maintain transparency, provide support, and manage expectations.

Recovery and Rebuilding

- **Assessing Financial Impact**: How to assess the financial impact of an economic disaster on personal finances and business operations. Discuss methods for evaluating losses, analyzing financial statements, and identifying areas for improvement.
- **Strategic Financial Recovery**: Strategies for recovering from an economic disaster,

including restructuring debt, rebuilding credit, and developing a long-term financial recovery plan. Discuss how to set realistic goals and track progress.

- **Rebuilding and Investment Opportunities**: Identifying opportunities for rebuilding and investing after an economic downturn. Discuss potential areas for growth, new business ventures, and investment strategies that align with changing economic conditions.

Long-Term Financial Resilience

- **Building Financial Resilience**: Strategies for building long-term financial resilience to better withstand future economic disruptions. Discuss diversifying income sources, investing in skills and education, and maintaining a strong financial foundation.
- **Advocacy and Policy Engagement**: Engaging in advocacy and policy efforts to support economic stability and recovery. Discuss how individuals and businesses can contribute to broader economic recovery initiatives and support policy changes.
- **Educational Resources and Networking**: Utilizing educational resources and networking opportunities to stay informed about economic trends and best practices. Discuss the value of ongoing learning, professional development,

and community engagement in financial resilience.

Maintaining Mental and Emotional Health

- **Managing Stress and Anxiety**: Techniques for managing stress and anxiety related to economic challenges, including mindfulness, relaxation exercises, and seeking professional support. Discuss the importance of mental health during financial crises.
- **Support Systems and Counseling**: Accessing support systems and counseling services to cope with the emotional impact of economic disasters. Discuss available resources, including financial counseling, mental health support, and community services.
- **Balancing Work and Personal Life**: Strategies for balancing work and personal life during economic challenges, including setting boundaries, maintaining a healthy work-life balance, and prioritizing self-care.

Staying Informed and Engaged

- **Monitoring Economic Trends**: How to stay informed about economic trends and developments that could impact personal and business finances. Discuss sources of information, including financial news, economic reports, and expert analyses.

- **Participating in Financial Education Programs**: Engaging in financial education programs to enhance knowledge and skills related to economic management. Discuss the benefits of attending workshops, webinars, and online courses.
- **Sharing Knowledge and Resources**: Sharing knowledge and resources about economic disaster preparedness and recovery with others. Discuss how community collaboration and information sharing can enhance overall resilience and support.

Chapter 13
Surviving Biological and Chemical Disasters

Understanding Biological and Chemical Disasters

- **Types of Biological Disasters**: Explanation of various biological disasters, including pandemics, bacterial outbreaks, and viral infections. Discuss their origins, modes of transmission, and impact on public health and safety.
- **Types of Chemical Disasters**: Overview of chemical disasters such as industrial spills, chemical attacks, and hazardous material leaks. Explain the potential sources, effects on human health, and environmental consequences.
- **Historical Examples**: Examination of historical biological and chemical disasters, such as the 1918 flu pandemic, the Ebola outbreak, and the Bhopal gas tragedy. Discuss the lessons learned and their relevance to current preparedness and response strategies.

Preparing for Biological Disasters

- **Health Precautions**: Steps for taking health precautions to prevent the spread of biological agents. Discuss vaccination, hygiene practices, and personal protective equipment (PPE) to reduce the risk of infection.
- **Emergency Medical Supplies**: Importance of maintaining an emergency supply of medical essentials, including medications, first-aid kits,

and personal protective gear. Provide guidelines for stocking and updating these supplies.

- **Contingency Planning**: Developing contingency plans for biological emergencies, including isolation procedures, quarantine protocols, and communication strategies. Discuss how to create a plan that addresses potential scenarios and ensures readiness.

Preparing for Chemical Disasters

- **Chemical Safety Practices**: Guidelines for practicing chemical safety in environments where hazardous materials are present. Discuss safe handling, storage, and disposal of chemicals, as well as emergency response measures.
- **Emergency Response Kits**: Creating and maintaining emergency response kits for chemical disasters, including containment materials, decontamination supplies, and protective clothing. Provide details on assembling and using these kits effectively.
- **Evacuation Procedures**: Developing and practicing evacuation procedures in case of a chemical disaster. Discuss how to plan evacuation routes, communicate with family members, and ensure safe evacuation from affected areas.

Responding to Biological Disasters

- **Recognizing Symptoms and Seeking Help**: Identifying symptoms of biological infections and knowing when to seek medical assistance. Discuss common signs of illness, how to access healthcare, and the importance of timely intervention.
- **Isolating and Quarantining**: Procedures for isolating infected individuals and implementing quarantine measures to prevent the spread of disease. Provide guidelines for setting up isolation areas and managing quarantine protocols.
- **Communication and Information Sharing**: Effective communication strategies for disseminating information about biological threats and health guidelines. Discuss how to use various communication channels to provide accurate and timely updates.

Responding to Chemical Disasters

- **Immediate Actions**: Steps to take immediately after exposure to chemical agents, including decontamination, seeking medical help, and reporting incidents. Discuss the importance of prompt action to minimize health risks.
- **Decontamination Procedures**: Detailed procedures for decontaminating affected individuals, equipment, and environments.

Discuss methods for cleaning, disinfecting, and ensuring that chemical residues are safely removed.

- **Coordinating with Authorities**: Working with emergency services, public health agencies, and environmental authorities during chemical disasters. Provide guidelines for effective coordination and reporting to ensure a comprehensive response.

Recovery and Rehabilitation

- **Medical Follow-Up**: Importance of medical follow-up after exposure to biological or chemical agents. Discuss routine check-ups, long-term health monitoring, and treatment options for potential long-term effects.
- **Environmental Cleanup**: Steps for environmental cleanup and restoration after a chemical disaster. Discuss the role of specialized teams, methods for assessing contamination, and processes for removing hazardous materials.
- **Community Support and Counseling**: Accessing community support and counseling services to address psychological and emotional impacts of biological and chemical disasters. Discuss resources available for mental health support and recovery.

Long-Term Preparedness and Resilience

- **Building Community Resilience**: Strategies for building community resilience to biological and chemical disasters. Discuss the importance of public education, community engagement, and collaborative planning.
- **Updating and Testing Plans**: Regularly updating and testing preparedness and response plans to ensure their effectiveness. Discuss the importance of drills, plan revisions, and continuous improvement.
- **Advocacy and Policy Involvement**: Engaging in advocacy and policy efforts to improve disaster preparedness and response at the local, national, and international levels. Discuss how individuals and organizations can contribute to policy changes and support disaster management initiatives.

Staying Informed and Educated

- **Monitoring Public Health Alerts**: Keeping up-to-date with public health alerts and advisories related to biological and chemical threats. Discuss sources of information, including health departments, international organizations, and news outlets.
- **Participating in Training Programs**: Engaging in training programs and workshops to enhance knowledge and skills related to

biological and chemical disaster response.
Discuss the benefits of professional
development and certification.

- **Sharing Knowledge and Best Practices**:
Sharing knowledge and best practices with
others to promote awareness and preparedness
for biological and chemical disasters. Discuss
the value of information sharing and
community collaboration.

Chapter 14
Surviving in Conflict Zones: Wars, Proxy Wars, and Battles

Understanding the Nature of Modern Conflicts
Modern conflicts, whether they be wars, proxy wars, or localized battles, are complex and multifaceted. Understanding the nature of these conflicts is crucial for survival.

Types of Conflicts

- **Wars:** Full-scale wars involve large-scale combat between nations or groups. These conflicts typically include conventional warfare with organized military forces, but may also involve asymmetric warfare tactics like guerrilla warfare or terrorism.
- **Proxy Wars:** These are conflicts where two or more external powers support opposing sides, often providing weapons, funding, or even troops. The Vietnam War and the Syrian Civil War are classic examples. In proxy wars, civilians may be caught in the crossfire or used as leverage by the conflicting powers.
- **Localized Battles:** These are smaller-scale conflicts, often within a city or region. They might not have the same global significance as a war, but they can be just as deadly for those living in the affected area. Examples include clashes between rival factions, gang wars, or uprisings.

Impact on Civilians

The impact of conflict on civilians is profound and devastating. In full-scale wars, entire cities can be destroyed, leading to mass displacement, loss of life, and destruction of infrastructure. In proxy wars, civilians may be targeted as a strategy to weaken the enemy. Localized battles can create zones of intense violence, making daily life impossible.

Civilians face a range of challenges, from being caught in crossfire to dealing with shortages of food, water, and medical care. The psychological toll of living in a conflict zone is immense, often leading to long-term trauma.

Psychological Effects:

Living in a conflict zone can lead to severe psychological issues such as PTSD, anxiety, and depression. The constant threat of violence, loss of loved ones, and the destruction of one's home can be overwhelming.

It's essential for individuals to recognize the signs of mental distress and seek help when possible, whether through community support, counseling, or, if available, professional mental health services.

Identifying and Responding to Early Warning Signs

Recognizing the early signs of conflict is vital for taking timely action to ensure personal safety.

Political Tensions and Unrest

Early warning signs of conflict often include escalating political tensions. This can manifest as increased government censorship, crackdowns on protests, or military mobilization. Understanding these signs can help you prepare for potential conflict.

Monitoring news reports, paying attention to government announcements, and observing the general mood in your community can provide critical information about the likelihood of conflict.

Media and Information

In the age of information, staying informed is key to survival. However, in conflict zones, misinformation and propaganda can be rampant. It's crucial to cross-check information from multiple sources and rely on trusted news outlets.

Social media can be both a blessing and a curse. While it can provide real-time updates, it can also spread panic through rumors. Learn to differentiate between credible sources and fake news.

Community Communication

Establishing and maintaining communication within your community is essential. Neighborhood watch groups or local networks can provide early warnings and share resources.
Consider setting up a system of communication that doesn't rely on the internet or mobile networks, which might be disrupted during conflict. Simple methods like whistle codes, flags, or hand signals can be effective.

Immediate Actions When Conflict Erupts
When conflict breaks out, immediate and decisive action can mean the difference between life and death.

Safety in Shelter

The first step during a conflict is to find a safe place to shelter. Ideally, this should be a location that is structurally sound, has minimal exposure to windows, and offers protection from bullets or shrapnel.
Underground bunkers, basements, or interior rooms with reinforced walls are preferred. If such options are unavailable, find the sturdiest part of your home and fortify it as much as possible.

Evacuation Planning

Evacuation might be necessary if the conflict escalates. Have a go-bag ready with essentials like water, non-perishable food, medical supplies, important documents, and communication devices. Pre-arrange meeting points with family or group members in case you get separated. Know multiple evacuation routes and be prepared to leave on short notice.

Communication

Maintaining communication with loved ones and authorities is critical. Use encrypted messaging apps to ensure privacy if you're in a high-risk area. Walkie-talkies or other radio devices can be lifesavers if the mobile network fails.
Keep a list of emergency contacts and local authorities. Establish a check-in system with family members to ensure everyone's safety.

Survival Strategies During Prolonged Conflict
Surviving a prolonged conflict requires careful planning and resource management.

Resource Management

Rationing is essential when supplies are limited. Divide your food and water into portions that can last for the maximum number of days. Store perishable items in cool, dark places to extend their shelf life.

Plan meals based on caloric needs and try to include foods that provide energy and nutrients. Avoid waste by reusing water when possible and repurposing food scraps.

Medical Emergencies

Conflict zones often lack adequate medical care. Knowing basic first aid can save lives. Learn how to treat wounds, manage infections, and perform CPR.

Keep a well-stocked first aid kit, including antiseptics, bandages, pain relievers, and any necessary prescription medications. Be aware of the signs of shock, dehydration, and other common issues.

Maintaining Morale

Mental resilience is just as important as physical survival. Engage in activities that boost morale, such as reading, journaling, or playing games. Maintaining a routine can provide a sense of normalcy.

Stay connected with your community for emotional support. Share stories, resources, and experiences to build a sense of solidarity.

Navigating the Aftermath of Conflict
After the conflict ends, rebuilding and recovery become the focus.

Dealing with Displacement

Displacement is a common consequence of conflict. If you've been forced to leave your home, finding temporary shelter is the first priority. Look for aid from humanitarian organizations that provide housing, food, and medical care.
Keep important documents safe and easily accessible. Register with local authorities to access services and support.

Rebuilding and Recovery

Rebuilding after conflict is a long and difficult process. Start by assessing the damage to your home and community. Prioritize essential repairs that make your living space habitable again.
Seek assistance from government programs, NGOs, and community initiatives that support rebuilding efforts. Pool resources with neighbors to tackle larger projects.

Legal and Social Challenges

Conflict often brings legal complications, such as property disputes, compensation claims, and war crimes. Understanding your rights is crucial for navigating these challenges.

Access legal aid if possible, and participate in community meetings to stay informed about post-conflict legal processes.

International Support and Humanitarian Aid
International support plays a critical role in recovery from conflict.

Role of NGOs and International Agencies

Organizations like the Red Cross, UNHCR, and Médecins Sans Frontières provide vital services during and after conflicts. They offer food, shelter, medical care, and legal assistance.

Understanding the structure and function of these organizations can help you access the aid you need.

Volunteer opportunities may also be available, allowing you to contribute to recovery efforts.

Accessing Aid

Learn how to navigate the aid distribution process. Register with local relief agencies, and stay informed about where and when aid will be distributed.

Be aware of potential challenges, such as corruption or mismanagement, and report any issues to the appropriate authorities.

Long-Term Rehabilitation

Recovery from conflict is a long-term process that involves rebuilding not just physically, but emotionally and socially as well. Access to mental health support, education, and vocational training is crucial for rebuilding lives.

Participate in community efforts to rebuild infrastructure, create jobs, and restore social services. Engage in dialogue and reconciliation processes to heal divisions caused by conflict.

Conclusion

As we conclude "The Ultimate Resilience Building Plans: A Practical Guide to Understanding and Surviving Disasters," it is crucial to reflect on the key themes and insights presented throughout the book. The journey through this manual has been designed to equip readers with the knowledge and tools needed to navigate the complexities of disaster preparedness and response effectively. This final chapter aims to summarize the essential takeaways and underscore the importance of continuous preparedness in ensuring safety and resilience.

The Importance of Comprehensive Preparedness

Throughout the book, we have explored a diverse range of disasters, from natural events such as hurricanes and earthquakes to man-made crises like industrial accidents,wars and terrorist attacks. Each chapter has provided detailed guidance on how to prepare for, respond to, and recover from these emergencies. The overarching theme is clear: effective disaster management requires a proactive and well-rounded approach. Comprehensive preparedness involves not only understanding the specific nature of each disaster but also implementing practical strategies that can be tailored to individual and community needs.

Key Takeaways

Understanding Risks: One of the foundational elements of preparedness is a thorough understanding of the potential risks and hazards specific to your location and circumstances. Identifying these risks allows for the development of targeted strategies and ensures that resources are allocated effectively.

Practical Planning: The manual emphasizes the importance of detailed planning, including the creation of emergency kits, evacuation plans, and communication strategies. These plans should be regularly reviewed and updated to reflect changing circumstances and new information.

Actionable Strategies: Each chapter has provided actionable steps and practical advice tailored to different types of disasters. These strategies are designed to be easily implemented and adaptable, ensuring that readers can effectively respond to emergencies as they arise.

Resilience and Recovery: Beyond immediate response, the manual highlights the significance of long-term recovery and resilience. This includes managing the emotional and psychological impacts of disasters, financial recovery, and the rebuilding process. Developing a resilient mindset and understanding the recovery process are crucial for bouncing back stronger after a disaster.

The Role of Community and Collaboration

Disaster preparedness and response are not solely individual responsibilities but involve collective efforts. Building strong community networks and fostering collaboration with local organizations and authorities can enhance the effectiveness of preparedness measures. Community involvement plays a vital role in ensuring that resources are shared, information is disseminated, and support systems are established.

Continuing Education and Adaptation

The landscape of disaster management is constantly evolving, with new risks emerging and best practices being refined. It is essential for readers to continue their education on disaster preparedness and adapt their plans as needed. Staying informed about new developments, participating in training exercises, and engaging with local disaster response initiatives are all important steps in maintaining preparedness.

Final Thoughts

The ultimate goal of this manual is to empower readers to take control of their safety and well-being in the face of disasters. By providing a comprehensive guide to understanding and surviving various emergency situations, the manual aims to instill confidence and preparedness in its readers. As you apply the knowledge and strategies outlined in this book, remember that preparedness is a continuous journey. Regularly review and update your plans, engage with your community, and stay informed to ensure that you are ready to face any challenge that may arise.

In closing, we hope that "The Ultimate Resilience Building Plans" serves as a valuable resource for you and your loved ones. May you find strength, resilience, and readiness as you navigate the complexities of disaster preparedness and response. Stay safe, stay prepared, and face the future with confidence.

++ THE END ++

9 798340 430526